A HOUSE AND A TEPEE

by Jane Manners
illustrated by Royce Fitzgerald

Harcourt

Orlando   Boston   Dallas   Chicago   San Diego

Visit *The Learning Site!*

www.harcourtschool.com

Homes can be different.

How are these homes
the same?
How are they different?

People can live in a tepee.
People can live in a house.

People lived in tepees
many years ago.
People lived in houses, too.

It takes time to make a
house like this.

It takes very little time to set up a tepee.

A tepee has one room.
A house can have many
different rooms.

Long ago, people had
to go for water.
Now we can get water
from a sink.

A house can keep a
family warm in winter
and fresh in summer.

So can this tepee.

What if the people wanted to move?

It was easy to move a tepee.
It's not easy to move a house!